976.6
JOH

CPS – MORRILL SCHOOL

Acres of aspiration.

W9-ATR-890

34880030035674

976.6
JOH

Johnson, Hannibal B.

Acres of aspiration.

C. 74

$26.95

DATE	BORROWER'S NAME	

976.6
JOH

Johnson, Hannibal B.

Acres of aspiration.

C. 74

$26.95

34880030035674

CPS – MORRILL SCHOOL
CHICAGO PUBLIC SCHOOLS
6011 S ROCKWELL STREET
CHICAGO, IL 60629
03/13/2006

BAKER & TAYLOR

Acres of Aspiration

THE ALL-BLACK TOWNS IN OKLAHOMA

Acres of Aspiration

THE ALL-BLACK TOWNS IN OKLAHOMA

Hannibal B. Johnson
Foreword by Michael Eric Dyson, Ph.D.
Cover Art by Clay Portis

EAKIN PRESS ◆ Austin, Texas

976.6
Joh
C.74
2004
26.95

For CIP
information,
please access:
www.loc.gov

FIRST EDITION
Copyright © 2002
By Hannibal B. Johnson
Published in the United States of America
By Eakin Press
A Division of Sunbelt Media, Inc.
P.O. Drawer 90159 ⏩ Austin, Texas 78709-0159
email: sales@eakinpress.com
💻 website: www.eakinpress.com 💻
ALL RIGHTS RESERVED.
1 2 3 4 5 6 7 8 9
1-57168-664-9 HB
1-57168-670-3 PB

Contents

Acknowledgments

Special thanks to the following for their assistance with various aspects of this project: Martin H. Belsky, Esq.; Lelia Foley-Davis; Cindy Driver; Michael Eric Dyson, Ph.D.; Bruce Fisher; Cassandra Gaines; Sharon Gallagher; Turner Goodrum; Ernest L. Holloway, Ph.D.; Kimberly Johnson; the Kansas State Historical Society; Robert Littlejohn; Joseph McCormick; Larry O'Dell; the Oklahoma Historical Society; Clay Portis; Loretta Radford, Esq.; Alisha L. Reynolds; Karen Rogers; Rudisill North Regional Library; Judy Eason-McIntyre; Nancy Sherbert; Rabbi Charles P. Sherman; Christie Stanley; Tuskegee University Archives; and the Western History Collections, University of Oklahoma Library.

Foreword

The Hunger for Home

The hunger for home has been a constant theme of black life. Since Africans were ripped from their native shores and brought to America in chains, the search for a place to call our own has ignited dreams of a black homestead. Through a succession of brutal displacements—from the slave field to the big house, from the plantation to the sharecropper's sullen sod—black folk have sought to ground our racial ambitions in friendly soil. Wherever we have laid our heads and rested our feet, the earth beneath us, and the sky above, have sprouted metaphors of nurture and belonging. Whether we planted our soles in "God's green earth" or raised our sights to "the heavens above," black folk have sought a sure sign that we were not owned, but owners. And hence, true citizens in a nation where we were once regarded as little more than pigs or horses.

But if the search for a home has fired the black imagination, the notion of mobility has been equally central to black progress. Black migrations have marked the restless hunt for respect that has seized black souls. Coerced migration from Africa was but the first of many forced flights that have flung the ambitions of blacks far beyond the geography we occupy. Land was always more than dirt with a design. It was also the symbolic possession of a people forever fleeing one plot for another, seeking to free themselves from the terror of enemies who wished to bury them beneath the mud of bigotry and hate. Black folk were always on the move, throwing off oppression like stifling clothes and inhabiting new land with old hopes of freedom. The great migration in the early twentieth century that shifted black bodies from the south to northern and western destinations renewed this hope.

But even before the great migration, black folk provided for their futures by planning all-black towns. Long before they were victimized by agrarian decline, marginalized by the industrial revolution and displaced by urban renewal—which often meant black removal—black folk created a space of community that resisted the suffocating apartheid of the South. Black entrepreneurs flourished and black homes, schools, and churches thrived when a black universe was taken for granted. These towns, largely located in the West, symbolized the blackening of an American frontier that had been largely reserved for whites. If the West was won by rural ingenuity and pioneering courage, then all-black towns were structured by black genius and racial fortitude.

Hannibal Johnson's *Acres of Aspiration* is an exemplary work that recovers a past buried beneath historical neglect and cultural ignorance. Johnson's beautifully written book gives us a compelling view of the struggles waged by black pioneers like Edward P. McCabe to enliven the black hope for home. By probing the outlines of the Oklahoman experiment in domestic stability, Johnson takes measure of the collective desire to stand tall on black soil. Moreover, his fine scholarly work uncovers the story of black self-determination that has too long been hostage to intellectual disinterest. His lucid narrative waves off naysayers to black achievement while bidding us to attend to the storied past of blacks caught in the long historical shadow of white heroes. If Johnson's book proves anything, it is that stirring acts of bravery were committed by everyday people saddled with illiteracy and burdened by white resistance. Yet they stayed the course and built towns as monuments to black survival.

Johnson's book is especially valuable for detailing the forces that drove the rise and fall of all-black towns. In the process, he gives us a political pamphlet as well as a historical script, since we gain insight into the economic factors and social drama that shaped the geography of black destiny. The denigration of blackness that drove blacks from land to land is depressingly up-to-date, if not in the sheer volume of race hatred that persists as in the vicious subtlety of anti-black sentiment. *Acres of Aspiration* gives new texture to the proposition that the past is prologue, since current claims to black reparations are grounded in the land, lives, and losses of black folk that Johnson so ably describes.

The timing of Johnson's book is particularly important in light of the terrorist acts committed against this nation on September 11, 2001. America is presently reeling in the face of the most heinous acts of subversion visited directly upon our soil in the nation's history. When two airplanes crashed into and then crumbled the twin towers of New York's World Trade Center, and another plane nose-dived into Washington, D.C.'s Pentagon, the terror that we had so long been exempt from, and that was common in other parts of the world, came crashing in on our lives. Now we are embroiled in a war against Afghanistan's ruling Taliban, even as we witness the rise of other acts of terror in our nation—especially with the weaponizing of anthrax in what appears to be biological warfare. The United States is caught in a nightmare of unreason bolstered by hate of the West and a history of American wrongdoing in the Middle East.

Johnson's book reminds us that black folk have lived with a long legacy of low-grade domestic terrorism. We have often been victimized by fellow citizens who claimed their terrorist acts—whether Ku Klux Klansmen burning crosses on black lawns, or aerial terrorists fire-bombing Tulsa, Oklahoma, in 1921—were motivated by the urge to cleanse the landscape of threatening forces. In truth, their terrorism was little more than the thinly veiled desire to contain, control, and destroy black life in the name of a racial ideology that mistook patriotism for nationalism. The former is the critical affirmation of one's country in light of its best values and social visions. It is enlightened support of the nation's political health through critical engagement and constructive critique. The latter is the uncritical devotion to one's country regardless of its political limitations and moral flaws. It counsels wholesale support of the nation without regard to ethical principles that supersede one's commitment to national self-interest. Black folk have been most patriotic when they loved their country enough to point out its failures in order to make it a better nation, such as Martin Luther King, Jr., did when he criticized the Vietnam War. Or as Oakland Congresswoman Barbara Lee did when she voted against giving President George W. Bush the power to go to war. In both cases, King and Lee were widely reviled. In light of King's subsequent vindication, perhaps Lee's singularly brave act will win her eventual recognition for her true patriotism. In any case, Johnson's book shows how bigots behave, sometimes in the name of patriotic duty, sometimes in the name of national self-interest.

Acres of Aspiration also shows just how heroic black folk have been in determining their own fate, and thus, enhancing the political health of the entire nation. When black folk built their own towns, they were not only helping themselves, but, ironically enough, helping to hold the nation together by resisting the tide of white supremacy. Instead of reacting with vengeance toward whites who drove them from their homes, blacks responded with edifying dignity and dug deep into the soil of black creativity to fashion towns that reflected their will to survive. In the process, blacks proved the very humanity that was called into question by racist whites. It is that humanity which is so vitally alive and generously displayed in Hannibal Johnson's engaging, insightful, and instructive book.

—MICHAEL ERIC DYSON, PH.D.
Author, Lecturer, and
Professor of Religious Studies
at DePaul University

Prologue

[T]he impossible is the least that one can demand—and one is, after all, emboldened by the spectacle of human history in general, and American Negro history in particular, for it testifies to nothing less than the perpetual achievement of the impossible.
—JAMES BALDWIN, *THE FIRE NEXT TIME*

Lyrics from a now classic African-American spiritual capture the essence of the Black experience in America: "Tell me how we got over, Lord. I've been falling and rising, all these years. You know my soul looks back and wonders, how I got over."[1]

Throughout the course of history, threats to the cultural identity and integrity of African-Americans sprang from many founts. Yet despite coerced immigration, slavery, lynching, peonage, sharecropping, segregation, discrimination, and more, African-Americans "got over" by maintaining an unshakable faith in a better place. That better place, sometimes earthly, sometimes ethereal, gave reason for hope.

Beulah Land. Paradise. Shangri-la. Oklahoma seemed to be all of these in the hostile, racist, post–Civil War South. In the end, it mattered less what these African-American seekers thought Oklahoma was, and more what they thought it was not:

> My relatives [came] to Oklahoma to get away from racism, violence, and death. In fact, my grandfather Guess just barely made it out of Tennessee alive. The night before he left Memphis, the mob came for him. But he had gotten word that the mob would be coming... [so he] fled to a neighbor's house where he was hidden until he could get safely out of Tennessee. If it had not

been for those kind, courageous neighbors, the mob would have lynched nine black men that night and I wouldn't be here today.[2]
—WILHELMINA GUESS HOWELL
(Born April 25, 1907, McAlester, Oklahoma)

The Black settlers' westward migration, fueled in equal measure by desperation and hope, riveted the nation. In the South, some bade them good riddance, seeing in their exodus a solution to the so-called "Negro problem." Others, largely plantation barons, discouraged the migration, seeking to keep the Negroes down on the farm as sharecroppers, mere peons in an agrarian system of economic bondage.

Like abolition before it and civil rights after it, the great "Black Exodus" represented a people's movement—an empowering, post–Civil War social movement with Black self-determination as its principal aim. Blacks sought to free themselves of the harsh post-Reconstruction backlash of serfdom and intimidation.

Beyond the natural yearning for freedom, many Blacks held firm to a perceived economic truth: land ownership held the key to success. Moreover, they thought land ownership would lead inexorably to full citizenship.

Despite an auspicious beginning, the all-Black town movement crested between 1890 and 1910, when American capitalism virtually completed the transition from rural agrarianism to urban industrialism.[3] Consequently, both the availability of land and the viability of small, independent enclaves diminished dramatically.

In trickles, then in torrents, Blacks streamed first into Kansas, then increasingly into Oklahoma. This bold swim upstream by Black pioneers sparked controversy, then fear and resentment, among local whites.

This decidedly mixed reception failed to stem the tide of migrants. The floodgates having parted, a cascade of newcomers spilled across the region. Oklahoma, some thought, would evolve into an all-Black state captained by a Black governor. All-Black towns and settlements in the windswept Oklahoma plains captured the collective imagination of an entire people.

All-Black enclaves served dual interests. First, such enclaves offered a real possibility of political participation free of the stinging, stifling oppression born of White dominance. Second, these all-

Black settlements encouraged Black land ownership by weaning disenchanted, disenfranchised Blacks from the bosom of the South.

A host of social and economic factors ultimately sealed the fates of these unique, historic oases. Many perished. Others faded. Only the strong survived. The few that remain serve as testaments to the human spirit and monuments to the power of hope, faith, and community.

To the pioneers who founded them—ordinary people who charted an extraordinary course—we remain endlessly indebted. We cannot blaze the trails to our future without first retracing the footsteps of our past.

Introduction

Behold, I have refined thee, but not with silver;
I have chosen thee in the furnace of affliction.
—ISAIAH 48:10

The twists and turns of the African-American roller coaster ride through American history date back at least to 1619. J. Saunders Redding, a Black writer, captures the essence of that singularly pivotal moment in time:

> Sails furled, flag drooping at her rounded stern, she rode the tide in from the sea. She was a strange ship, indeed, by all accounts, a frightening ship, a ship of mystery. Whether she was a trader, privateer, or man-of-war no one knows. Through her bulwarks black-mouthed cannon yawned. The flag she flew was Dutch; her crew a motley. Her port of call, an English settlement, Jamestown, in the colony of Virginia. She came, she traded, and shortly afterwards was gone. Probably no ship in modern history has carried a more portentous freight. Her cargo? Twenty slaves.[1]

From the beginning, it became clear that the ride would be anything but joyous. Wrenched from motherland, culture, and family, a harrowing journey lay in wait. Eartha Colson's poignant poem "Tears of the Atlantic" reminds us of what the African captives endured and how they managed somehow to overcome:

> Souls overboard......Souls overboard
>
> You can kill the body
> But you can't kill the soul
> The soul lives on

You can kill the body
But the soul lives on

Thousands boarded vessels
headed for this western world

Sickness and disease
Cast overboard souls

The Atlantic cries
African tears
of African souls

Tears of the Atlantic
The Atlantic cries for me

Souls overboard......Souls overboard
The Atlantic cries for me

The journey's long
the weak discarded
the women raped

Sick overboard
My mother overboard
My father overboard
My sister overboard
My brother overboard

You can kill the body
But you can't kill the soul
The soul lives on

The Atlantic still cries
African tears
of African souls
The Atlantic cries for me[2]

First herded, then packed like freight in the dark, dank holds of foreign seafaring vessels, these American slaves-to-be wallowed in filth and choked on fetid air. Even those who survived the treacherous voyage paid a terrible price both physically and psychologically. Documents from the era describe the wretched conditions:

The height, sometimes, between decks, was only eighteen inches; so that the unfortunate human beings could not turn around, or even on their sides, the elevation being less than the breadth of their shoulders; and here they are usually chained to the decks by the neck and legs. In such a place the sense of misery and suffocation is so great, that the Negroes ... are driven to frenzy.[3]

Remarkably, many of the expatriated Africans survived the horrendous conditions of the transport. Yet landfall provided no safe haven; slavery afforded no solace.

The slave narratives provide a rich oral history of the day-to-day lives of these forced immigrants. Collected through oral interviews in the mid- to late 1930s, the stories paint an unimaginably bleak and deeply disturbing portrait.[4] Extraordinary inhumanity and cruelty became ordinary—routine, regimented, and institutionalized.

Modern-era atrocities like the European Holocaust attest to our continuing capacity to ignore the great moral lessons of history. Indeed, Ann Birstein and Alfred Kazin, in a reader's supplement to *Anne Frank: The Diary of a Young Girl*, refer to "the heartlessness, the bestiality, the still unbelievable cruelty of the Germans in World War II."[5] No less can be said of American slavemasters and the institution of slavery itself. Consider the following excerpts from the Texas volume of the slave narratives:

My mama belong to old William Cleveland and old Polly Cleveland, and they was the meanest two white folks what ever lived, 'cause they wal allus beatin' on their slaves ... Old Polly, she was a Polly devil if there ever was one, and she whipped my little sister what was only nine months old and jes' a baby to death. She come and took the diaper offen my little sister and whipped till the blood jes' ran—jes' 'cause she cry like all babies do, and it kilt my sister. I never forgot that, but I got some even with that old Polly devil and it's this-a-way.

You see, I's 'bout ten year old I belongs to Miss Olivia, what was that old Polly's daughter, and one day old Polly devil comes to where Miss Olivia lives after she marries, and trys to give me a lick out in the yard, and I picks up a rock 'bout as big as half your fist and hits her right in the eye and busted the eyeball, and tells her that's for whippin' my baby sister to death. You could hear her holler for five miles, but Miss Olivia, when I tells her, says, 'Well, I guess Mama has larnt her lesson at last.' But that old Polly was mean like her husban', and I hopes they is both burnin' in torment now. [6]

—MARY ARMSTRONG

Massa never 'lowed us slaves go to church, but they have big holes in the fields they gits down in and prays. They done that way 'cause the White folks didn't want them to pray. They used to pray for freedom.

When the White folks go off they writes on the meal and flour with they fingers. That the way they know if us steal meal. Sometime they take a stick and write in front of the door so if anybody go out they step on the writin' and massa know. That the way us larn how to write.

Old mass didn't give 'em much to eat. When they comes in out of the field they goes work for other folks for something to eat. [7]

—ELLEN BUTLER

Let 'em ketch you with a gun or a piece of paper with writin' on it and he'd whip you like everything. Some of the slaves, if they ever did git a piece of paper, they would keep it and learn a few words ... You would think they was going to kill you, he would whip you so if he caught you with a piece of paper. [8]

—AUSTIN GRANT

Old Marse bad. He beat us till we bleed. He rub salt and pepper in. One time I sweep de yard. Young miss come home from college. She slap my face. She want to beat me. Mama say to beat her, so dey did. She took de beatin' for me. [9]

—AGATHA BABINO

Despite mind-numbing drudgery, daily indignities, and unspeakable hardships, these uprooted Africans persevered. Moreover, they managed to project to their masters a gleeful insouciance that defied the rigors of their pitiful existence. Many a slave simply wore a mask, as African-American poet Paul Laurence Dunbar describes:

· 4 ·

We wear the mask that grins and lies,
It hides our cheeks and shades our eyes,
This debt we pay to human guile;
With torn and bleeding hearts we smile,
And mouth with myriad subtleties.
Why should the world be otherwise,
In counting all our tears and sighs?
Nay, let them only see us, while
    We wear the mask.

We smile, but O great Christ, our cries
To thee from tortured souls arise.
We sing, but oh, the clay is vile
Beneath our feet, and long the mile;
But let the world dream otherwise,
    We wear the mask.[10]

Of the mythical "happy slave," the oxymoron used to justify maintaining the status quo, John Little, a former slave, wrote:

They say slaves are happy, because they laugh, and are merry. I myself and three or four others, have received two hundred lashes in the day, and had our feet in fetters; yet, at night, we would sing and dance, and make others laugh at the rattling of our chains. Happy men we must have been! We did it to keep down trouble, and to keep our hearts from being completely broken: that is as true as the gospel! Just look at it,—must not we have been very happy? Yet I have done it myself—I have cut capers in chains.[11]

The slave mask hid searing pain. Individual slaves would be bloodied, but as a people, Blacks would be unbowed. Fired in this crucible of hardship and suffering, a remarkable and enduring resilience of spirit emerged.

Prodigious author and acerbic social critic James Baldwin, in *The Fire Next Time*, spoke of the ironically redemptive power of Black suffering:

This past, the Negro's past, of rope, fire, torture, castration, infanticide, rape; death and humiliation; fear by day and night, fear as deep as the marrow of the bone; doubt that he was worthy of life, since everyone around him denied it; sorrow for his women, for his kinfolk, for his children, who needed his protection, and whom he could not protect; rage, hatred, and murder, hatred for white men so deep that it often turned against him and his own, and made all love, all trust, all joy impossible—this past, this endless struggle to achieve and reveal and confirm a human identity, human authority, yet contains, for all its horror, something very beautiful. I do not mean to be sentimental about suffering—enough is certainly as good as a feast—but people who cannot suffer can never grow up, can never discover who they are. That man who is forced each day to snatch his manhood, his identity, out of the fire of human cruelty that rages to destroy it knows, if he survives his effort, and even if he does not survive it, something about himself and human life that no school on earth—and, indeed, no church—can teach. He achieves his own authority, and that is unshakable. This is because in order to save his life, he is forced to look beneath appearances, to take nothing for granted, to hear the meaning behind the words. *If one is continually surviving the worst that life can bring, one eventually ceases to be controlled by a fear of what life can bring; whatever it brings must be borne.*[12] [Emphasis added.]

As much as anything else, this great survival instinct coupled with an unyielding sense of hope for a brighter future formed the backdrop for the creation of the so-called "all-Black towns" in America.

Brooklyn, Illinois, lays claim to being the oldest Black town in America.[13] The town's motto, "Founded by Chance, Sustained by Courage," speaks volumes.[14] Brooklyn began as a collective of a few "freedom villages" established by fugitive slaves and free Blacks. Founders incorporated the community as a municipality in 1873, four years prior to the founding of Nicodemus, Kansas, one of the better-known all-Black towns in the United States.[15] Most all-Black towns dotted the western frontier or, like Mound Bayou, Mississippi, lined the rustic South.[16] Brooklyn emerged in an urban industrial complex. Still, the underlying rationales for their formation and, to a large degree, the challenges they all faced, are strikingly similar.

These towns arose primarily as a solution to the "Negro problem" and proliferated in Oklahoma. Ironically, decades earlier, President Andrew Jackson and others proclaimed Oklahoma—literally "land of the red people" in the Choctaw language—the solution to the "Indian problem."[17] Jackson signed the Indian Removal Act into law on May 28, 1830:

> So obsessed was the president with driving the Indian tribes to the far frontiers of the United States that he gave his personal attention to the matter. It is significant that most of the Indian removals [to Oklahoma] took place during his administration and that those not completed before he left office had been set in motion. The fulfillment of the Jackson removal program, with its ruthless uprooting and prodigal waste of Indian life and property to satisfy the president's desires and demands of his constituency, has been aptly described as the "Trail of Tears."[18]

The Jacksonian philosophy underlying the Indian removal program—that an "Indian problem" existed instead of a problem with the Indians—flew in the face of the American ideal of equality. This view minimized and denigrated the worth and dignity of an entire people. Post-Reconstruction Blacks, the source of the so-called "Negro problem," understood this "us versus them" mindset. As scapegoats themselves, they fully appreciated the tyrannical power of the majority. They removed themselves to all-Black towns, thereby circumventing the forcible removal that their parents, grandparents, and, more recently, their Indian kin, endured.

All-Black towns symbolized a new sense of race consciousness. After a 1908 visit to Boley, one of Oklahoma's surviving Black towns, legendary educator and statesman Booker T. Washington wrote:

> [T]he ... Negro towns that have sprung up represent a dawning of race consciousness, a wholesome desire to do something to make the race respected: something which shall demonstrate the right of the Negro, not merely as an individual but as a race, to have a worth and permanent place in the civilization that the American people are creating.[19]

Many shared Washington's outward-focused desire to garner White respect. Yet another, more subtle, consideration underlay the formation of all-Black towns. Though less often articulated, all-Black towns served an inward-focused function. They enhanced a fragile, collective Black psyche damaged immeasurably by years of bondage, peonage, and maltreatment. All-Black towns, then, became tangible proof of self-worth.

Washington conceived of all-Black towns as laboratories for a grand social experiment. He found in their success corroboration for his hypothesis that Black Americans, given opportunity, could succeed economically. In Washington's view, the reward for such proof crystallized into a single word—*respect*, a commodity long denied his people:

> The wisest among my race understand that the agitation of questions of social equality is the extremist folly, and that progress in the enjoyment of all the privileges that will come to us must be the result of severe and constant struggle rather than of artificial forcing. No race that has anything to contribute to the markets of the world is long in any degree ostracized. It is important and right that all privileges of law be ours, but it is vastly more important that we be prepared for the existence of these privileges. The opportunity to earn a dollar in a factory just now is worth infinitely more than the opportunity to spend a dollar in an opera house.[20]

Many Black nationalists of the era shared the Washingtonian view that the economic progress of the race would, in time, guarantee political progress. Thus, in the minds of subscribers to this philosophy, creating self-governing Black towns would garner from Whites a level of respect commensurate with demonstrable evidence of industriousness. With that enhanced respect would come a diminution in Black suffering and, eventually, a broadening of Black rights.

Ultimately, a number of pernicious social ills—most notably, systemic, institutional racism—blunted the potential of this idealized social hypothesis. Yet through it all, African-Americans exhibited remarkable resilience. Commenting on this phenomenal triumph of the human spirit among African-Americans, Dr. Martin Luther King, Jr., in his *Letter from Birmingham Jail*, wrote:

For more than two centuries our forebears labored in this country without wages; they made cotton king; they built the homes of their masters while suffering gross injustice and shameless humiliation—and yet out of a bottomless vitality they continued to thrive and develop. If the inexpressible cruelties of slavery could not stop us, the opposition we now face will surely fail.[21]

Oklahoma's all-Black towns constitute a vital part of the legacy of the forebears of whom Dr. King spoke. All told, Oklahoma boasted more than fifty Black towns and settlements in the pre-statehood "Twin Territories": Oklahoma Territory and Indian Territory.

What particular factors prompted the establishment of these towns? Who inhabited them? Where did the migrants originate? Who backed and boosted them? How did their existence impact social, economic, and political relations between and among the races? How did they ultimately fare? What is the status of the remaining towns? What are their prospects for survival?

Black presence in Oklahoma dates back at least as far as the six-teenth century, when Blacks accompanied Spanish explorers to the area.

Oklahoma was once considered as the site of an all-Black state. Senator Henry W. Blair of New Hampshire introduced a bill in favor of the proposal.

In 1879 Blacks migrated in large numbers from the South to Kansas and other parts of the Midwest.

Many Blacks prospered in Oklahoma as members of the various Native American tribes.

Black freedmen in Oklahoma were known as "Natives," while Black immigrants from other areas, particularly the South, were called "Watchina" or "State Negroes."

Hannibal C. Carter helped establish the Freedmen's Oklahoma Immigration Association in Chicago in 1881.

Some of the "Sooners" who came to Oklahoma in the great land run of 1889 were Black.

Historically, Oklahoma boasts more all-Black towns than any other state.

1.

The Push for an All-Black State

In the great struggle now progressing for the freedom and elevation of our people, we should be found at work with all our might,
resolved that no man, or set of men shall be more abundant in
labors, according to the measure of ability, than ourselves.

—FREDERICK DOUGLASS

The Status of Pre-Emancipation Blacks

Pre-emancipation America, even for "privileged" Blacks, left
much to be desired. The United States Supreme Court, in the still-
infamous *Dred Scott* decision, lent its imprimatur to slavery. The
court held that the United States Constitution protected slavery in
the states as well as in the territories. Moreover, Blacks had no legal
standing in the courts of the United States of America, no institutional platform from which to challenge their bondage. *Dred Scott*
left little room for hope:

It is difficult at this day to realize the state of public opinion in relation to that unfortunate race, which prevailed in the civilized and enlightened portions of the world at the time of the Declaration of Independence and when the Constitution of the United States was framed and adopted.... They had for more than a century before been regarded as beings of an inferior order, and altogether unfit to associate with the white race, either in social or political relations, and so far inferior, that they had no rights which the white man was bound to respect.[1]

Celebrated historian Dr. John Hope Franklin offers a similarly bleak assessment of the precarious condition of mid–nineteenth century Blacks:

The terrible truth is that by the beginning of the Civil War the status of free black persons had deteriorated to the point that they were pariahs of the land, unwanted, virtually helpless, and with no substantial basis for relief or redress of grievances under the Constitution.[2]

The world took note of their plight. Viewed from a more global perspective, America seemed incapable of spanning her monumental racial chasm. French journalist and social commentator Alexis de Tocqueville, in *Democracy in America* (1835), perceived a great and insurmountable racial divide:

I do not imagine that the white and black races will ever live in any country upon an equal footing. But I believe the difficulty to be still greater in the United States than elsewhere. An isolated individual may surmount the prejudices of religion, of his country, or of his race, and if this individual is a king he may effect surprising changes in society; but a whole people cannot rise, as it were, above itself. A despot who should subject the Americans and their former slaves to the same yoke, might perhaps succeed in commingling their races; but as long as the American democracy remains at the head of affairs, no one will undertake so difficult a task; and it may be foreseen that the freer the white population of the United States becomes, the more isolated will it remain.[3]

Even Abraham Lincoln, the "great emancipator," equivocated on the issue of Black equality prior to his presidency. In his 1858 campaign in Illinois for the United States Senate against Stephen Douglas, Lincoln fashioned his rhetoric as follows in Chicago:

Let us discard all this quibbling about this man and the other man, this race and that race and the other race being inferior, and therefore they must be placed in an inferior position. Let us discard all these things, and unite as one people throughout this land, until we shall once more stand up declaring that all men are created equal.[4]

Just a mere two months later, speaking in the southern Illinois town of Charleston, he refashioned his position:

I will say, then, that I am not, nor ever have been, in favor of bringing about in any way the social and political equality of the white and black races [applause]; that I am not, nor ever have been, in favor of making voters or jurors of negroes, nor of qualifying them to hold office, nor to intermarry with white people....

And inasmuch as they cannot so live, while they do remain together there must be the position of superior and inferior, and I as much as any other man am in favor of having the superior position assigned to the white race.[5]

Even after his ascent to the highest office in the land, President Abraham Lincoln privately acknowledged remarkable indifference on the question of Black liberation:

My paramount object in this struggle is to save the Union ... If I could save the Union without freeing any slave I would do it; and if I could save it by freeing all the slaves I would do it; and if I could save it by freeing some and leaving others alone I would also do that. What I do about slavery, and the colored race, I do because I believe it helps to save the Union....[6]

Though equality remained a distant hope, Blacks eventually gained some measure of freedom. The issuance of the Emancipation Proclamation in 1863, the passage of the Thirteenth Amendment to the United States Constitution in 1865, and the signing of post–Civil War treaties in 1866 between the federal government and the Five Civilized Tribes calling for the abolition of tribal slavery signaled progress.

But Blacks realized that mere manumission would be woefully insufficient. The attainment of education, political rights, and economic clout would necessitate pit stops along the long, winding road to true equality. Racism would emerge as a series of capricious but recurrent roadblocks.

Asked by General William Sherman in 1865 whether they preferred to live scattered among Whites or in separate enclaves, twenty Black leaders responded emphatically that, in light of chronic racial prejudice, they preferred to live in separate communities. To be sure, they longed for quality education and political suffrage, but economic clout took precedence. Land ownership became the top priority. Indeed, Blacks laid claim to land entitlements based upon their blood, sweat, and tears as slaves and their unremitting valor in service to the country during the Civil War.[7]

With one exception, the government rejected these claims. Only freed tribal slaves eventually received land rights. Land allotments typically ranged between forty and one hundred acres.[8]

Following the Civil War, the United States House of Representatives entertained bids by Radical Republicans like Charles Sumner, Thaddeus Stevens, and George W. Julian to confiscate land from the southern planter class and distribute it to newly freed Blacks in forty-acre lots.[9] With seeming prescience, the uncharacteristically visionary lawmakers argued that the failure to grant land to the freedmen would result in a permanent underclass of oppressed, exploited, and powerless Black serfs in a feudal-like agrarian system.[10]

Fellow lawmakers snuffed out the so-called "forty acres and a mule" bill. Opinion-shapers such as the New York Times newspaper and The Nation magazine joined the chorus of opposition to the measure.[11] The year was 1866. The final tally on the "forty acres and a mule" bill: 126 opposed; 37 in favor.[12]

Yet another glimmer of hope for Blacks in the economic arena came from another federal government initiative. The government created the Freedmen's Savings and Trust Company, better known as the "Freedmen's Bank," in 1865. Designed to assist freedmen in the transition from slavery to freedom and give Blacks economic clout, the Freedmen's Bank debuted to great excitement. By the end of 1865, there were ten branches; by 1872 there were thirty-four, thirty-two of which served southern states. By 1874 total deposits in the Freedmen's Bank amounted to $3,299,201. But careless bookkeeping, incompetence, improvident lending policies, and corruption ran rife. Losses mounted. Even the assumption of the role of Freedmen's Bank president by statesman Frederick Douglass in 1874 and his personal $10,000 loan to the institution could not forestall its failure. The Freedmen's Bank closed. Depositors, after long delays, received less than fifty cents on the dollar. For Blacks, both faith in fellow man and faith in saving suffered mighty blows.[13]

Other prominent economic issues loomed. Though slavery had ended, the southern power elite orchestrated variations on that cruel theme. Among them, peonage and sharecropping struck particularly dissonant chords.

Under peonage, a Black man would be arrested for "vagrancy," a trumped-up charge that essentially amounted to unemployment. He would be ordered to pay a fine that he could not afford, then incarcerated for non-payment. A "White knight" plantation owner would pay the fine, in essence lending the jailed man enough money to set himself free. The plantation owner would then "hire" the now-released Black man until the indebtedness could be repaid. The peon would be forced to work, locked up at night, and dogged by bloodhounds should he have the gall to run away. Slaves had been of considerable monetary value to plantation owners. Peons, lacking such value, suffered gross mistreatment up to and including murder at the hands of plantation owners, at little cost to the latter.[14]

Soon, an insidious system of sharecropping evolved in the South. Free Blacks worked as sharecroppers for plantation owners, often their former masters. They lived in squalid quarters on the plantation, worked in exchange for part of the crop, and bought goods from the plantation store. Dealings in cash were rare.

With remarkable consistency, Black workers lived at a subsistence level, often barely able to pay off their debts. The following transactional ledger recording the relationship between a Black sharecropper, Polly, and the plantation owner for whom she worked, Presley George, illustrates this never-ending economic quagmire:

Due Presley George by Polly:

For 4¾ cuts of wool @ 75 cents/cut	$ 3.50
22 yds. Cloth @ 50 cents/yd.	11.00
5 yds. Thread @ 50 cents/yd.	2.50
Boarding one child (who didn't work) for 5 months	12.00
10 bushels corn @ $1.00/bushel	10.00
30 bushels corn @ $1.00/bushel	30.00
TOTAL	$69.00

Due Polly by Presley George:

For 3 months' work "by self" @ $4.00/month	$12.00
For 4 months' work by son Peter @ $8.00/month	32.00
For 4 months' work by son Burrel @ $4.00/month	16.00
For 4 months' work by daughter Siller @ $2.25/month	9.00
TOTAL	$69.00[15]

A nineteenth-century folk song laments the dilemma Blacks faced just after emancipation:

> Slabery an' freedom
> Dey's mos' de same
> No difference hahdly
> Cep' in de name.[16]

Historian Lerone Bennett, Jr., in *Before the Mayflower*, recounted the findings of General Carl Schurz, special investigator for President Andrew Johnson. Schurz described the horrid state of affairs most southern Blacks faced even after the end of legally sanctioned servitude.

> "Some planters," [Schurz] said, "held back their former slaves on their plantations by brute force." Armed bands of white men patrolled the country roads to drive back the Negroes wandering the highways and by-ways. Gruesome reports came from the hospitals—reports of colored men and women whose ears had been cut off, whose skulls had been broken by blows, whose bodies had been slashed by knives or lacerated with scourges. A number of such cases I had occasion to examine myself. A ... reign of terror prevailed in many parts of the South.

Lynch victim—a Black man lynched by a mob.
—Courtesy the Western History Collections,
University of Oklahoma Library

Throughout this period, and on into the 1870s, hundreds of freedmen were massacred in "riots" staged and directed by policemen and other governmental officials. In the Memphis, Tennessee, "riot" of May, 1866, forty-six blacks (Union veterans were a special target) were killed and seventy-five were wounded. Five black women were raped by whites, twelve schools and four churches were burned. Two months later, in New Orleans, policemen returned to the attack, killing some forty blacks and wounding one hundred.

"The emancipation of the slave," General Schurz concluded, "is submitted to only in so far as chattel slavery in the old form could not be kept up. But although the freedman is no longer considered the slave of society ... [w]herever I go—the street, the shop, the house, the hotel, or the steamboat—I hear the people talk in such a way as to indicate that they are yet unable to conceive the Negro as possessing any rights at all. Men who are honorable in their dealings with their white neighbors will cheat a Negro without feeling a single twinge of their honor. To kill a Negro, they do not deem murder; to debauch a Negro woman, they do not think fornication; to take property away from a Negro, they do not consider robbery."[17]

In the face of this open hostility to the freedmen, even in spite of the passage of the Thirteenth Amendment, Congress again amended the United States Constitution with the passage of the Fourteenth Amendment in 1866 and the Fifteenth Amendment in 1870.

The Thirteenth Amendment already provided:

Section 1. Neither slavery nor involuntary servitude, except as punishment for crime whereof the party shall have been duly convicted, shall exist within the United States, or any place subject to their jurisdiction.

Section 2. Congress shall have the power to enforce this article by appropriate legislation.[18]

Now the Fourteenth Amendment added, in pertinent part:

Section 1. All persons born or naturalized in the United States, and subject to the jurisdiction thereof, are citizens of the United States and of the State wherein they reside. No State shall make or enforce any law which shall abridge the privileges or immunities of citizens of the United States; nor shall any State deprive any person of life, liberty, or property, without due process of law; nor deny to any person within its jurisdiction the equal protection of laws.

. . .

Section 5. The Congress shall have the power to enforce, by appropriate legislation, the provisions of this article.[19]

And the Fifteenth Amendment further provided:

Section 1. The right of citizens of the United States to vote shall not be denied or abridged by the United States or by any State on account of race, color, or previous condition of servitude.

Section 2. The Congress shall have power to enforce this article by appropriate legislation.[20]

These measures promised the Negro full citizenship rights as a matter of law. Progress, it was believed, had come at long last. Ebullient Blacks found much cause for celebration in this period unparalleled in the nation's history:

Never before had the sun shone so bright. A former slave named Blanche Kelso Bruce was representing Mississippi in the United States Senate. Pickney Benton Stewart Pinchback, young, charming, daring, was sitting in the governor's office in Louisiana.

In Mississippi, South Carolina, and Louisiana, black lieutenant governors were sitting on the right hand of power. A black was secretary of state in Florida; a black was on the state supreme court in South Carolina. In these and other Southern states, blacks were superintendents of education, state treasurers, adjutant generals, solicitors, judges and major generals of militia. Robert H. Wood was mayor of Natchez, Mississippi, and Norris Wright Cuney was running for mayor of Galveston, Texas. Seven blacks were sitting in the House of Representatives.

Nor was this all. Blacks and whites were going to school together, riding on streetcars and cohabiting, in and out of wedlock. An interracial board was running the University of South Carolina, where a black professor, Richard T. Greener, was teaching white and black youth metaphysics and logic.[21]

But as quickly as progress had been achieved, it would begin to stall.

The First Wave: "The Great Negro Exodus to Kansas"

The federal government withdrew troops from the South in 1877, effectively halting Reconstruction-era gains in race relations.[22] Blacks sought a way out of increasingly oppressive conditions. The migration northward thus began.

The fervent push for an all-Black enclave in Oklahoma took root in neighboring Kansas. That state witnessed, during the period from roughly 1879 through 1881, a mass influx of eager Blacks from the South. These "Exodusters" fled unrelenting terrorism and oppressive economic conditions, seeking safe haven in what they believed to be the Beulah Land in Kansas.[23] Black-nationalists-turned-promoters like Henry Adams and Benjamin "Pap" Singleton, a Tennessee-born former slave and self-styled "Black Moses," seduced the restless multitudes with flowery literature and soaring oratory. And the people responded with their feet—some 40,000 of them. John B. Van Deusen, in an article entitled "The Exodus of 1879," published in the *Journal of Negro History*, noted:

The movement centered the attention of the North on the supposed wrongs of the Southern Negro and collections were taken at public meetings to promote emigration. The halls of Congress rang with denunciations of the Southern Egyptians whose hard hearts compelled the freedmen to leave the land of their birth for the New Northern Canaan. In 1880 the Senate of the United States appointed a committee to investigate the exodus, and nearly seventeen hundred printed pages were filled with testimony.

Although various factors were involved in the exodus, three causes stand out prominently: (1) a sense of personal insecurity attending the reversion of the South to Democratic rule and political discontent among the blacks resulting from disfranchisement; (2) economic discontent resulting from low prices for cotton and the system of debt-servitude which grew out of the operation of the crop lien system; and (3) attractive propaganda. This consisted in part of circulars advertising the holdings of certain land-grant railroads and in part excitement worked up by local leaders. Discrimination in the courts and inadequate educational facilities were sometimes mentioned as causes....[24]

Renowned African-American author Richard Wright, in the conclusion of his book *Black Boy*, expresses the motivation behind his own South-to-North migration decades later. Wright's lyrical explication seems an equally apt characterization of many Exodusters:

> I was taking a part of the South to transplant in alien soil, to see if it could grow differently, if it could drink of new and cool rains, bend in strange winds, respond to the warmth of other suns, and, perhaps, to bloom. ... I headed North, full of a hazy notion that life could be lived with dignity, that the personalities of others should not be violated, that men should be able to confront other men without fear or shame, and that if men were lucky in their living on earth they might win some redeeming meaning for their having struggled and suffered here beneath the stars.[25]

Blacks dotted the bucolic landscape in Kansas hamlets such as Leavenworth, Wyandotte, Kansas City, and Topeka. However, a bitter, brutal winter during 1879–80 left scores of these trailblazers with inadequate food, clothing, and shelter. As word of the harsh conditions spread, the migration to Kansas tapered off.[26]

Most prominent Black leaders of the day, including Henry H.

Garnet, Sojourner Truth, Richard T. Greener, John M. Langston, and George T. Downing, endorsed this massive diaspora from the South. One did not: Frederick Douglass, abolitionist, journalist, and statesman. With time, Douglass argued vehemently, the morally superior position of full equality for Blacks would hold sway in even the recalcitrant South. He thus advocated fight over flight. The "fight" he envisioned amounted to a moral struggle of unspecified duration and, in the eyes of many, of uncertain outcome.

> Douglass... was an inveterate optimist. He firmly believed that the righteousness of the Negro's cause in concert with the enlightened and progressive tendencies of the day ensured that conditions would improve; that one day soon, the Negro would really be free. The ultimate rule of moral law certified Douglass's optimism. He argued that "while revolutions may for a time seem to roll backwards; while reactionary tendencies and forces may arrest the wheels of progress, and while the colored man of the South may still have to suffer the lash and sting of a by-gone condition, there are forces and influences silently and yet powerfully working out his deliverance." He added that "the individual Southern States are great, but the nation is greater. Justice, honor, liberty and fidelity to the Constitution and Laws may seem to sleep, but they are not dead."
>
> Moreover, in light of the immense obstacles that freedpeople endured in their continuing struggle for freedom, Douglass contended that to complain of their apparent lack of progress was both unjust and uncalled for. He countered: *"the wonder is, not that the freedmen have made so little progress, but, rather, that they have made so much—not that they have been standing still, but that they have been able to stand at all."*[27] [Emphasis added.]

Douglass's protestations against Black emigration notwithstanding, a sense of unbounded optimism prevailed. Kansas became a Midwest siren, luring thousands of Blacks to what they thought would be Shangri-la. White Kansans, alarmed by the rapid "browning" of the state, soon became less than hospitable hosts. Racial tension flared.

Just as the allure of Kansas began to fade, the Indian country to the south—Oklahoma—beckoned. Yet another odyssey would ensue, and this time the stakes would be higher.

Oklahoma: The Early Migration

The initial foray of African-Americans into what is now Oklahoma dates back to 1541 when they arrived with Spanish explorers. That year, Francisco de Coronado led thirty of his soldiers on a gold-seeking expedition through what would become America's forty-sixth state. Subsequent expeditions by the French, then the Native Americans, brought more Blacks to Oklahoma.[28]

Oklahoma's identity as a state cannot be separated from its Native American roots. Yet throughout the course of the young state's history, Oklahoma's Native American and African-American populations shared cultural experiences and blood lineage. L. J. Abbott observed, in his 1907 article in *The Independent* magazine entitled, "The Race Question in the 46th State":

> You can offend a black no easier than by denying his Indian parentage. This is so ... thruout Oklahoma. Every negro that can possibly maintain his contention insists that he is an "Indian." In this way he feels that he can avoid some of the antipathy that meets his race at every turn.
>
> [I]t must be confessed that the negro Indian ... does occupy a more influential position in Oklahoma society than the mulatto or the pure-blood African. This can partially be explained from the fact that [negro Indians] have large landed interests, and that they are a decided factor in the politics of the new State. But the stain of negro blood in their veins puts a social barrier upon all the tribe.
>
> . . .
>
> I know of a Creek, who, so far as one could judge by appearances, is a White man. He undertook to prove his Indian blood in the Creek courts so as to be allotted land in severalty. The investigation developed the fact that he was one-sixteenth negro and had no Creek blood at all. Immediately his wife left him, his business was ruined, he was a marked man, with no future other than the future a negro of intelligence and capacity can hope for within that race. That woman would have had to accept the social position of a Creek negro had she remained that merchant's wife. As it was, her children had a stain that soap would not wash out, nor society forgive, in the South.[29]

The Creek Council, 1900. Top row, left to right: John Yargee, Lewis Adams, John C. Weeks, George W. Adams, James Sapulpa, Timmie Fife. Middle row, left to right: Legus C. Perryman, Joseph Henry Land, William A. Sapulpa, Thomas C. Adams. Front row, left to right: J.C. Heydrick, Creek Indian (unidentified).

—Courtesy the Western History Collections, University of Oklahoma Library

Even today, many African-Americans in Oklahoma proudly admit of Native American blood, some a small degree, others a significant percentage.

Indeed, many of Oklahoma's earliest Black settlers in this third-wave migration accompanied members of the so-called Five Civilized Tribes on their forced migration from the southeastern states in the 1830s and 1840s. On this ghastly "Trail of Tears"—a death march for many—Black slaves and some free Blacks marched with the Chickasaws, Choctaws, Cherokees, Creeks, and Seminoles, slaveholders all. Dale Van Every, in his book *The Disinherited*, described it this way:

> The long somber columns of groaning ox wagons, driven herds and straggling crowds on foot inched on westward through swamps and forests, across rivers and over hills, in their crawling

struggle from the lush lowlands of the Gulf to the arid plains of the west. In a kind of death spasm one of the last vestiges of the original Indian world was being dismembered and its collapsing remnants jammed bodily into an alien new world.[30]

The long walk to Oklahoma complete, surviving Native Americans faced conditions that only exacerbated their woes. Unfamiliar climatic conditions, fertile but uncultivated Indian Territory soil, a lack of farm tools, malaria and other unfamiliar diseases, and depression and anxiety born of separation from ancestral lands devastated these new Oklahomans. For example, among the Creeks, the population plummeted from 24,000 to 13,500 in fewer than twenty-five years.[31]

Ironically, for Black Creeks—slaves, tribal members, and their descendants—the migration from the southeast proved fortuitous. In the period during which the Indian population among the Creeks declined by 50 percent, the number of Black Creeks quadrupled.[32]

Having escaped the rabidly racist South, Black Creeks viewed Oklahoma as something akin to the Promised Land. They thrived.[33]

Black Creek freedmen, so-called "Natives," grew accustomed to many of the privileges of full citizenship among the Indians. These Natives, having been in Oklahoma for years, would come to resent the onslaught of new Black migrants from the South who arrived later in the nineteenth century. They saw the migrants, whom they called "Watchina" or "State Negroes," as too servile, too willing to kowtow to whites. On his refusal to meet with new Black migrants, a Creek freedman pointedly observed: "I was eating out [of] the same pot with the Indians ... while they was still licking the master's boots in Texas."[34]

Slaves living among the Indian tribes attained freedom pursuant to post–Civil War treaties. The Civil War proved economically and politically devastating for the Indian tribes. Under Reconstruction, the Union meted out punishment for official tribal allegiance to the Confederacy, as evidenced by several 1861 treaties that had been signed with Confederate agents. Negotiations between the Union and the tribes began in Fort Smith, Arkansas, in 1865 and concluded in Washington, D.C., in 1866. Under the final agreements, the Five Civilized Tribes acquiesced to federal conditions that required them to: (1) abolish the institution of slavery; and (2) surrender a large portion of Indian Territory in central and western Oklahoma—"Oklahoma Territory"—to be used as the removal relocation site for the Kansas tribes.[35]

Another important stipulation of the postwar treaties effectively obliterated Indian Territory. Indian nations agreed to permit the right-of-way for, at a minimum, a north-south and an east-west railroad through their sovereign lands. The north-south franchise went to the Missouri, Kansas, and Texas (MKT or "Katy") Railroad. The Atlantic and Pacific, later known as the St. Louis and San Francisco ("Frisco") Railroad, secured the east-west privileges. Railroads begot commerce. Commerce attracted people.[36] Wherever the railroads went, eager settlers followed not far behind. Black freedmen emerged among those who pioneered new villages, towns, and cities in Oklahoma.

The disparate treatment of freedmen among the Indian tribes sparked federal concern. The Creeks and Seminoles considered the freedmen to be their equals. They supported full citizenship for freedmen in their respective tribes. Some of the Cherokees wanted the freedmen moved outside tribal lands to their own separate habitat. Others, including the principal chief of the Cherokee Nation, advocated for retaining the freedmen within tribal lands, but in a segregated area. The Choctaw and Chickasaw nations grudgingly and gradually acceded to the realities of emancipation, but not without incident. Prejudice against and violence toward Blacks ran rampant. After the Civil War, the Choctaw and Chickasaw nations banned from tribal re-entry Black Union Army veterans. The Choctaws and Chickasaws had backed the Confederate Army in the Civil War.[37]

Under the 1866 treaties executed by each of the tribes, the Creeks, Seminoles, and Cherokees stipulated to full citizenship rights for freedmen. The Choctaws and Chickasaws did not. The freedmen, feeling betrayed by the latter tribes, sought federal protection of their rights.[38]

Even as the Indian tribes began to adjust to the new theoretical reality of Black equality, Whites increasingly viewed Oklahoma as their potential new home. Their aggressive homesteading efforts further reduced Indian lands. Texas cattle ranchers took Cherokee land in western Oklahoma for grazing, first by adverse possession, then by treaty. Soon, railroad lobbyists, having already secured Oklahoma rights-of-way for their clients, began to press Congress for the opening of Oklahoma to White homesteaders. The demands for White settlement of Oklahoma burgeoned. The so-called "Boomers," led by explorer David L. Payne, made several unauthorized, yet highly publicized, excursions into Oklahoma in the early 1880s.[39]

The United States government nonetheless seemed to be an ally to Black migrants. Voicing concern about the tribes' pledge to extend tribal rights to the freedmen, the government contemplated the creation of an all-Black settlement zone or colony in central Oklahoma for the freedmen from the Five Civilized Tribes and from tribes in Kansas, other western states, and the territories.[40] The federal government's acquisition of Oklahoma Territory seemed to further this prospect.

Though the notion of a Black settlement zone for freedmen swirled around for some two decades, it never quite materialized. On the one hand, White homesteaders began to ratchet up their efforts to open these lands for the "Boomers." On the other, impassioned Black nationalists sought the opening of Oklahoma Territory to the broader group of disaffected Blacks from the South and the nation at large. Leading this charge, Hannibal C. Carter

Morris Shepard, a freedman.
—Courtesy the Archives & Manuscripts Division of the Oklahoma Historical Society

Edward P. McCabe while serving as assistant auditor of Oklahoma Territory.

—From the Oklahoma State Capitol Art Edition of May 26, 1900, courtesy the
Archives & Manuscripts Division of the Oklahoma Historical Society

helped establish the Freedmen's Oklahoma Immigration Association in Chicago on March 15, 1881, to colonize thousands of Black freedmen in Oklahoma Territory.[41]

The Freedmen's Oklahoma Immigration Association disseminated a circular from St. Louis in 1881 to the freedmen of the United States. The dispatch proclaimed that the federal government, anticipating the necessities of newly freed Blacks, had, in 1866, entered into treaties with the Creek, Seminole, and Chickasaw Indians that called for a cession of 14,000,000 acres on which to locate other Indians and Black freedmen. A newspaper commented:

> The Freedmen's Oklahoma Association has been formed in St. Louis. The association promises every freedman who will go to Oklahoma 160 acres of land free, and it is said too that agents have been sent into the Southern states to start an emigration movement to the Indian Territory among the colored people. The Freedmen's association bases its claim to entry on the lands of the Indian Territory on the treaties of 1866, made by the government with the Creeks and Seminoles.[42]

James Milton Turner, a Black Missouri promoter of the Oklahoma colonization movement, claimed that thousands of Blacks from Missouri prepared to enter the Oklahoma Territory in the spring of 1881.

Any hope of a successful mass Black settlement in the Oklahoma Territory soon faded, however. The secretary of the interior, Samuel J. Kirkwood, asked the commissioner of the general land office, Curtis W. Holcomb, to review whether and, if so, to what extent, Black freedmen had rights to settle in the Oklahoma Territory pursuant to the 1866 treaties with the Five Civilized Tribes. Holcomb concluded unequivocally that only those former Black slaves of the Indian tribes had such treaty rights:

> The treaty stipulations, as uniformly understood and construed, have no application to any other freedmen than the persons freed from Indian bondage. They relate exclusively to friendly Indians and to Indian freedmen of other tribes in the Indian Territory whom it was the desire of the United States to provide with permanent homes on the lands ceded for that purpose.
> The "freedmen of the United States" are not comprehended

within the policy of intention of the treaty provisions, and said lands have accordingly not "been purchased for the use and occupation" of the colored people of any of the States.

The present attempt to make use of the colored people of the country in the same direction, by deluding them with fictitious assurances that new and congenial homes can be provided for them within this Territory, deserves special reprobation, since its only effect must be to involve innocent people in a criminal conspiracy, and to subject them to disappointment, hardship, and suffering.[43]

In 1881 Judge Isaac C. Parker, presiding over the federal court for the western district of Arkansas in Fort Smith, Arkansas, ruled on the matter. Parker, appointed to the bench in 1874, maintained the largest criminal jurisdiction of any federal court in the land, covering western Arkansas and Indian Territory. He championed education reform, women's suffrage, Indian rights, and improvement of jail conditions. Though personally opposed to the death penalty, he ironically earned the nickname "The Hanging Judge" when, in accordance with the law he was sworn to uphold, he sentenced 160 people to the gallows, 87 of whom (including four women) were actually hanged.[44]

Judge Parker's ruling echoed Holcomb's restrictive reading of the Indian treaties' provisions regarding freedmen. Judge Parker held: "[C]olored persons who were never held as slaves in the Indian country, but who may have been slaves elsewhere, are like other citizens of the United States, and have no more rights in the Indian country than other citizens of the United States."[45]

Despite these monumental setbacks, Black nationalists continued to press for a Black settlement zone in the Oklahoma Territory. Indeed, on April 27, 1882, they convened in Parsons, Kansas, for a strategic planning session. The forty-five delegates assembled claimed to represent up to 60,000 blacks. Emboldened by the conference, they vowed to lobby Congress for the establishment of an all-Black state.[46] They ultimately achieved limited success.

Senator Henry W. Blair of New Hampshire introduced a bill in favor of creating a Black state. But Hiram Price, commissioner of Indian affairs, rebuffed the notion, telling Hannibal C. Carter, president of the Freedmen's Oklahoma Association, that the federal government reserved the lands for Indian freedmen only. Not dissuaded, Black nationalists continued their relentless agitation for an all-Black state for freedmen from throughout the South. Still, the government did not flinch. A subsequent commissioner of Indian affairs, I. D. Atkins, took the same stance as had his predecessor. His 1886 letter indicated that Oklahoma Territory would not be opened to freedmen generally, but would be limited to those freedmen who had been held by the Indian tribes.[47]

Finally, the persistence of the Boomers all but doomed the dreams of an all-Black state. Ranchers settled in the Oklahoma Territory in the 1870s and 1880s. Farmers also coveted the land. A groundswell of publicity about the Oklahoma Territory fueled letters to congressmen from Whites seeking to have the area opened for general settlement. Then, a series of rapid-succession decisions responded to these mounting pressures. The prospects for an all-Black state plummeted precipitously.

The federal government completed the purchase of Oklahoma Territory from the Creek and Seminole nations in early 1889. A March 1889 rider to the Indian appropriations bill opened the "unassigned lands" of Oklahoma Territory to general settlement. Just weeks thereafter, President Benjamin Harrison proclaimed that the public lands in Oklahoma Territory would be opened to settlers at noon on April 22, 1889.[48] Prior to the official opening, Black troops known as "Buffalo Soldiers" helped keep intruders and interlopers out of the area.[49]

The Oklahoma land run of 1889 brought some 50,000 "Sooners" to Oklahoma, including a number of Blacks. Some 6,000 Blacks called Indian Territory in Oklahoma home by 1870. By 1890 there were some 3,000 Blacks in Oklahoma Territory and approximately 18,000 in Indian Territory. By 1900 about 19,000 Blacks lived in Oklahoma Territory and 38,000 in Indian Territory.[50]

Despite discouraging, dispiriting setbacks along the way, hopes of carving out an all-Black enclave within Oklahoma endured. Murat Halstead, a leading Black nationalist of the era, discussed the significance of creating such an all-Black state within Oklahoma:

> It would afford the colored people a rallying point, a land of actual liberty and equality, a place where they could develop according to their capacity, where there would be none to molest and make them afraid; and there is no question of the importance

of the popularity of the movement. A single incident will do much to aid this tendency. It is that *William Waldorf Astor* has proposed to give a half a million dollars for the establishment of a colored university in Oklahoma, and in addition to this endowment will give $100,000 for buildings.

It is not only possible, but probable, that this is the beginning of a solution of the question of the races, the most important and dangerous question for the people of the United States. The boundaries of Oklahoma, if they should prove insufficient for the rush of the black population, would no doubt be enlarged by the action of the general governments, with the concurrence of the States immediately interested. With a black state, populous, prosperous, enlightened and honored, there would be an added dignity to the colored citizen, an increase of self-respect, and an end to the sense of subordination, injustice and helplessness which has been so injurious to the race.[51]

The "problem of the color line," as famed scholar, writer, and political activist W. E. B. Du Bois called it, permeated the collective psyche of the country.[52] Ironically, segregation—willful, deliberate, and self-imposed—seemed to offer Blacks a glimmer of hope on an otherwise gloomy American horizon. As Du Bois astutely observed: "There is in this world no such force as the force of a man determined to rise."[53]

Leading the charge to test the segregation supposition would be Edward P. McCabe, a Halstead contemporary. McCabe, an ambitious politician, real-estate speculator, and developer from Kansas, became the leading booster of separate all-Black settlements, first of an all-Black state, then of all-Black Oklahoma towns.

McCabe was for a time the highest-ranking Black elected state official in Kansas, serving two terms as state auditor (1882–86).

McCabe was a prominent, popular member of the Republican Party in both Kansas and Oklahoma.

McCabe lived for a time in Nicodemus, Kansas, one of the early and prominent all-Black towns.

Two Black ministers, William Smith and Thomas Harris, conceived the idea of creating an all-Black town in Nicodemus, Kansas.

McCabe came to Oklahoma in 1889 at the time of the great land run.

McCabe founded Langston, Oklahoma, and the *Langston City Herald* newspaper, a propaganda vehicle to encourage migration to the town.

In 1890 McCabe visited with President Benjamin Harrison, intent on convincing him of the wisdom of creating an all-Black state in Oklahoma.

When Oklahoma became a state in 1907, the first official legislative act was the passage of rigid "Jim Crow" laws. McCabe filed a lawsuit against such measures.

McCabe died a pauper in Chicago on February 23, 1920.

McCabe is buried in Topeka, Kansas.

2.

Edward P. McCabe: Father of the All-Black Town Movement

When a man raises himself from the lowest condition in society to the highest, mankind pays him the tribute of their admiration; when he accomplishes this elevation by native energy, guided by prudence and wisdom, their admiration is increased; but when his course ... proves a possible ... what had hitherto been regarded as an impossible ... then he becomes a burning and shining light, on which the aged may look with gladness, the young with hope, and the down-trodden, as a representative of what they may themselves become.

—James McCune Smith

Pioneer in the Promised Land

In the late nineteenth century and early twentieth century, the Black population swelled in Oklahoma, due in large measure to visionary "boosters" like Edward Preston McCabe. McCabe, an enormously popular, fair-skinned, straight-haired Black man of extraordinary intelligence and political instincts, crafted his success from the most humble of beginnings. Born in October of 1850 to poor parents in Troy, New York, McCabe and his family moved frequently. His schooling began in Fall River, Massachusetts, and continued in Newport, Rhode Island. After the untimely death of his father, McCabe worked as a brokerage-firm clerk and a part-time porter in New York City to help support his widowed mother and two siblings.

Finding opportunities for Blacks limited in New York, McCabe migrated west to Chicago. There, he worked as a clerk at the Palmer Hotel. McCabe also garnered an appointment as a clerk in the Cook County treasurer's office, becoming the first Black man to work in that office. Within the short span of two years, McCabe relocated still farther west to Nicodemus, Kansas, a much-heralded Black colony in Graham County.[1]

Nicodemus, started by two Black ministers from Clarksville, Tennessee, became a magnet for disaffected southern Blacks. The founders named the town for an African sold into slavery who purchased his freedom in the United States.[2]

Trekking westward in search of land in 1877, William Smith and Thomas Harris landed in Nicodemus, then teamed with a White land speculator, W. R. Hill, to promote the town. In summer of 1877, the first wave of Black migrants reached the town. Within two years, some 700 persons, scattered over seventy-two square miles, had arrived. The town boasted thirty-five houses, two churches, and one store. Of the original 149 families, a majority came from the Lexington, Kentucky, area.[3]

Life in early Nicodemus proved precarious. Wild animals, vermin, prarie fires, and crop failures drove some settlers back to the South. The faithful, those who stuck it out, suffered additional trials and tribulations before attaining a modicum of stability and success.

A promotional circular for Nicodemus, posted on July 2, 1877, boasted of the town's promise:

TO THE COLORED CITIZENS OF THE UNITED STATES.

Nicodemus, Graham Co., Kan., July 2d, 1877.

We, the Nicodemus Town Company of Graham County, Kan., are now in possession of our lands and the Town Site of Nicodemus, which is beautifully located on the N. W. quarter of Section I, Town 8, Range 21, in Graham Co., Kansas, in the great Solomon Valley, 240 miles west of Topeka, and we are proud to say it is the finest country we ever saw. The soil is of a rich, black, sandy loam. The country is rather rolling, and looks most pleasing to the human eye. The south fork of the Solomon river flows through Graham County, nearly directly east and west and has an abundance of excellent water, while there are numerous springs of living water abounding throughout the Valley. There is an abundance of fine Magnesian stone for building purposes, which is easier handled than the rough sand or hard stone. There is also some timber; plenty for fire use, while we have no fear but what we will find plenty of coal.

. . .

NICODEMUS.

Nicodemus was a slave of African birth,
And was bought for a bag full of gold;
He was reckoned a part of the salt of the earth,
But he died years ago, very old.

Nicodemus was a prophet, at least he was as wise,
For he told of the battles to come;
How we trembled with fear, when he rolled up his eyes,
And we heeded the shake of his thumb.

CHORUS: Good time coming, good time coming,
Long, long time on the way;
Run and tell Elija to hurry up Pomp,
To meet us under the cottonwood tree,
In the Great Solomon Valley
At the first break of day.[4]

E. P. McCabe arrived in May of 1878. He and his friend Abram T. Hall, former city editor of the *Chicago Conservator,* joined a party of immigrants on a two-day train-and-wagon procession to the town.[5] From the moment of arrival, Hall began having doubts. First, he stumbled into an unpleasant encounter with a rattlesnake. Then, his throat parched, he resorted to chewing garlic to quench his thirst. Finally, hungry and in need of fuel with which to cook, he turned to an "alternative" fuel—cow chips.[6]

McCabe, sophisticated and refined, found Kansas even more uninviting. "Roughing it" in the wild, wild West proved most unappealing to a man of his exquisite deportment. McCabe, Hall later recalled, sat in nauseated, stunned silence as he and others voraciously consumed their cow-chip-fired delicacies.[7]

The two men for a time shared a sod house and worked as government surveyors. Then Hall returned to Illinois to continue his career as a journalist.[8]

In Nicodemus, McCabe became a rising star in Republican Party politics. Recognizing his potential, then-governor St. John appointed the ascendant McCabe county clerk. From that point forward, the dashing and erudite McCabe drew statewide attention.

> At his party's convention in Leavenworth, in August, 1882, McCabe was placed in nomination as state auditor, and received it by acclamation. Here is how he was nominated by another delegate: "Mr. Chairman, I desire to place in nomination for the position of auditor a young man ... well and favorably known to you all; one who is not only popular with his own race but is exceedingly popular with the whites (great applause); the ablest and strongest colored man from a political standpoint in the state, the recognized leader of the race in the West (applause). His name is Edward P. McCabe. Nominate him and you will please the colored element of the party and a majority of whites ... I move that the rules be suspended and Mr. McCabe nominated by acclamation."
>
> The delegate's motion was seconded and put by the chairman, and then McCabe was nominated by acclamation amid thundering applause. Men arose and swung their hats, and yelled for McCabe.
>
> By an overwhelming vote, largely white, McCabe won that nomination and the following election. He also won the election of 1884.[9]

The people's selection of the "thirty-something" McCabe as state auditor in 1882 marked a milestone: no Black person had ever occupied such a high political office in the state of Kansas. Nonetheless, some exhibited obvious hostility toward the breaking of this longstanding, seemingly impenetrable, racial barrier. T. J.

Pickett, in a vituperative piece in the paper he edited, the *Kirwin Chief*, described McCabe as a "shrewd, unscrupulous, impudent fellow, without character or moral standing."[10] Even in the face of such *ad hominem* attacks, McCabe stood tall in the minds of the general public, Black and White.

McCabe served for two terms—four years in all—as auditor in Kansas, during which time he, his wife Sarah, and their daughter, Edwarda, lived in Topeka. He withdrew his name from contention for a third term as state auditor of Kansas when, in 1886, the mood of the Kansas Republican Convention shifted decidedly in favor of term limits. Even the governor, John A. Martin, remarked that he felt it improper for a public servant to aspire to more than two terms. Ever astute, McCabe saw racial hostilities as the subtext underlying the decline of his political fortunes. Pragmatically, but with great reluctance, he acquiesced to the crystal-clear wishes of his party's leadership. He chose not to seek a third term. Though neutralized politically, McCabe maintained his ties to Kansas until 1889.[11]

As his political fortunes in Kansas ebbed, news that settlers could legally enter Oklahoma Territory buoyed McCabe. He then set his sights on the land just to the south, the new frontier.

Native American habitation of and dominance in Indian Territory in Oklahoma went largely unchallenged. But Oklahoma Territory spelled opportunity, being for all practical purposes *terra nullius*—country belonging to no one. Seeing the Oklahoma land run of 1889 as a boon for Blacks generally, and a potential gold mine for himself, McCabe trekked to Oklahoma.

McCabe arrived in Guthrie, the Oklahoma territorial capital, with two White friends on the first day of the Oklahoma land run, April 22, 1889. His political acumen not the least bit diminished, he eventually became the first treasurer of Logan County. President Benjamin Harrison rewarded McCabe, a Republican Party loyalist, with an appointment to the position of deputy territorial auditor. He held the office until statehood, serving during both the term of the fourth territorial governor, Cassius M. Barnes, and the one-year tenure of Governor William A. Jenkins.[12]

Early in 1890, McCabe began a lucrative career in land speculation, promoting the Black town of Langston, forty miles northwest of Oklahoma City. He dubbed Langston, a town that derives its name from John H. Langston, a Reconstruction-era Black Virginia congressman, "The Only Distinctively Negro City in America."[13] Within two years, 1,700 town lots ranging in price from $10 to $50 had been sold. McCabe, who by then operated a real-estate office, the McCabe Townsite Company, acquired an additional 160 acres and divided it into small farming plots, which he then sold.

McCabe established the *Langston City Herald* in October of 1890 as a propaganda vehicle to promote the town. The weekly newspaper attracted some 600 subscribers. He also dispatched agents to the South to attract Blacks to his new utopia. He offered a real-estate contract, entitling the signatory to a railroad ticket to Guthrie, located just twelve miles from Langston, and a choice from among existing and available lots.[14] McCabe's grand vision called for the creation of an all-Black state within the Oklahoma Territory—a state which he, as governor, would lead.

While others bandied about similar notions. McCabe concretized his unadulterated idealism and unabashed self-interest into positive action:

> It is reported here that the Kansas radicals are trying to work a scheme to coax the negroes of that state to emigrate in a body to Oklahoma. The principal part of this scheme is the appointment of a man named McCabe, who was formerly auditor of the State of Kansas, Governor of Oklahoma when the bill passes Congress erecting the region into a territory. The belief of the Republican bosses is that if a negro is appointed Governor of Oklahoma, the negroes will flock not only from Kansas, but other parts of the country and try and capture that country and make it a negro state.
>
> It is no secret that the white Kansans are getting very tired of their negro fellow citizens and are anxious also to get rid of them. McCabe was elected auditor of Kansas at a time when the average Kansans only knew of the negro by hearsay. Since then, there has been a very considerable immigration of negroes to Kansas and it is entirely safe to say that a negro would now stand no chance of capturing a State office in that land of liberty and light. The Kansas negroes have been trying to break into the white schools and white churches and the offices that Kansans thought were created for the white man's pleasure and benefit. In consequence, there has been a good deal of friction. Kansas Republicans, from Ingalls down, believe it is entirely just and proper that negroes should hold the office in Mississippi and boss

that State, but they shudder at the idea that the negro should hold office in Kansas or have any voice in the conduct of the affairs of that State. McCabe has been here since March last trying to get some recognition, which of course means office, from the Harrison Administration. He was a member of the late negro Congress here, and pretended to represent Oklahoma, although he never saw that region and had no credentials from anybody there. He is a candidate for Governor of Oklahoma when that bill passes Congress and all of the Kansas Republicans are his supporters.

It is no secret that their object, in supporting him is to get him out of the State, and at the same time they are hoping that a good portion of the negroes will follow him to Oklahoma and erect that region into a negro commonwealth. The Oklahoma bill passed the Senate today with an amendment tacking on No-Man's-Land [the Oklahoma panhandle] to the territory now embraced in Oklahoma. It is probable that the Senate bill will be adopted by the House, perhaps with some modifications, and then Harrison will be called upon to appoint territorial officers, and will have a chance to show his love for the negro when McCabe's papers for Governor are before him.[15]

Newspapers far and wide caught wind of McCabe's bold gambit. Excerpts from a February 28, 1890, piece in the *New York Times* canvass the uneven topography of American public opinion:

TO MAKE A NEGRO STATE

Topeka, Kansas, February 27. An official just returned from Oklahoma, says there is much bitterness over the candidacy of Edward P. McCabe, colored, for Governor of that Territory. He declares emphatically that if President Harrison appoints McCabe Governor, the latter will be assassinated within a week after he enters the Territory. There is rapidly growing an anti-negro sentiment caused by the aggressiveness of the blacks wherever they are strong. This feeling bids fair to unite the whites irrespective of party.

· · ·

The negroes of Oklahoma, Kansas, Missouri, and portions of the South are urging the appointment of McCabe. Mr. McCabe was Auditor of the State of Kansas for two terms and has been looked upon by his people as a leader. The present movement is the first public action taken by a secret political organization which has for its avowed purpose the advancement of the negro in morals and in social standing. It also has in view the securing of control of Oklahoma, by Presidential aid, if possible, and if that cannot be brought about, by a general exodus of negroes to the new territory.

. . .

They propose to found a negro state, in which the white man will only be tolerated because of his business qualifications. The Brotherhood [The First Grand Independent Brotherhood] will fill all state, county, and municipal offices, if their dreams are fulfilled, and they now seem likely to be, they will have only negro school teachers, compel mixed school attendance, and demand full social equality from such Whites as love of money will bring to citizenship ... [.][16]

Just days later, yet another article about the proposed "Negro state" appeared in the *New York Times*. The March 1, 1890, piece noted: "If the black population could be distributed evenly over the United States it would not constitute a social or political danger. But an exclusively or overwhelmingly Negro settlement in any part of the country is, to all intents and purposes, a camp of savages."[17]

McCabe visited Washington, D.C., in March of 1890. There, he conferred with the twenty-third president of the United States, Benjamin Harrison, in a bid to gain approbation for his "Black state" proposition. In attempting to make his case, he urged that Oklahoma Territory would be perfectly suited for an all-Black state and that he would make an ideal inaugural governor. Intrigued by McCabe's audacious proposal, a perplexed President Harrison questioned why Blacks had chosen Oklahoma as opposed to a Southern state for the fulfillment of their nationalistic aspirations. Quick-witted McCabe replied:

We desire to get away from the associations that cluster about us in the Southern States. We wish to remove from the disgraceful surroundings that so degraded my people, and in the new territory in Oklahoma show the people of the United States and of the world that we are not only loyal citizens, but that we are capable of advancement, and that we can be an honor to those who owned us as chattels, but disavowed us as sons and daughters. We are willing to abide by that decision, but in a new country, on new lands, with a climate suited to our race, we desire to show you that we are men and women capable of self-government and loyal enough to add strength to the Government.[18]

McCabe's account of the abhorrent conditions facing southern Blacks hit the mark. In 1890 at least eighty-five Blacks were lynched in America, mostly in the South. The "Mississippi Plan," developed at the 1890 Mississippi State Constitutional Convention, laid the foundation for the disenfranchisement of Black southern voters through the imposition of poll taxes, literacy measures, and other qualification schemes. It swept the South. The United States Supreme Court, in a series of decisions, disenfranchised Black voters and sanctioned rigid segregation measures.[19] For Blacks, southern living was tantamount to not living at all.

President Harrison made no formal reply to McCabe's entreaty. A contemporaneous press account, however, suggests that the president seriously entertained McCabe's timely and impassioned plea:

[McCabe]... had a very satisfactory conference with the President in relation to Oklahoma matters. He is endorsed by many leading Republicans and is bringing strong local influence to bear. His candidacy for Governor is supported by the various colored colonies that have settled in Kansas and Oklahoma and by Republicans generally in the State, who argue that while there is no such thing as [setting] apart any given territory for any class of citizens, black or white, yet the appointment by the President of a representative colored man as Governor of Oklahoma would create such an immigration of colored people from the North and South to that Territory as to very soon give them absolute political control, and give the colored people an opportunity to show to the world their ability in building up a new State, in filling its offices and directing its political destinies. It is further claimed that the colored people are entitled to this consideration from the Republican Party, and that they would surprise the nation with the rapid development of the country and their knowledge of statecraft. The climate and soil of the territory lying west of the Arkansas River, including the entire Indian Territory, Oklahoma and the northern horn of Texas to the Rio Grande River is large enough for three or four States, and is peculiarly adapted to cotton, tobacco, corn, sorghum and stock raising. With proper encouragement, it is believed that 50,000 colored people can be directed to Oklahoma during the year 1890.[20]

While awaiting official Washington's action on his gubernatorial aspirations, McCabe continued to appeal to Black frustration with second-class American citizenship as a means to promote migration to Oklahoma. McCabe's compare-and-contrast bulletins juxtaposed southern oppression with Oklahoma opportunity:

> What will you be if you stay in the South? Slaves liable to be killed at any time, and never treated right: but if you come to Oklahoma you have equal chances with the white man, free and independent. Why do Southern whites always run down Oklahoma and try to keep the Negroes from coming here? Because they want to keep them there and live off their labor. White people are coming here every day.[21]

The uncertainty surrounding the prospect of an all-Black state did not detract from the plausibility of smaller-scale Black nationalistic zones: Black towns. McCabe's determination to keep the town of Langston Black led to extraordinary, though not wholly novel, measures. For example, McCabe attempted to include restrictive covenants in land titles to prevent the transfer of property to Whites.[22] Whites, of course, utilized such tactics to keep Blacks out long before—and long after—this era.

The few White families that settled in early Lansgton moved out when the town of Coyle sprang up. Its namesake, a White Langston resident, lost a bid to build a wholesale house in Langston. When the Santa Fe Railroad could not reach agreement with Langston leaders on a right-of-way through town, Coyle, already disgruntled, arranged for a suitable right-of-way just three miles east. The all-White town of Coyle was born.[23]

Colonists in early Langston, often lured by overblown advertisements and grandiose rhetoric, frequently met with disappointment. The *Langston City Herald* painted a picture of a prettified, idyllic community. The reality simply did not jibe with the puffery. In its infancy, Langston consisted of a single general store, wooden shacks, and a mass of tents. Residents awaited the construction of real homes. Indeed, in 1891 a reporter for the *New York Times* found two hundred people living in Langston, some with only the clothes on their backs, many hungry. Men in Langston plowed an eighty-three-acre cooperative garden plot to feed the needy.[24] To his credit, McCabe warned migrants to come prepared for the harsh conditions that might initially befall them. But he buried most of his warnings in obscure footnotes in broad-brush appeals for Black migration. Some—unprepared, struggling, and feeling deceived—returned to the South.

Still, others came. They came by rail. They came by wagon. They came by foot. Many of the migrants hailed from Arkansas, Texas, and the "Deep South," where they steadfastly worked the soil. McCabe, in an 1892 edition of the *Langston City Herald,* proclaimed: "Real estate is the basis of all wealth." The paper also boldly asserted that Oklahoma spelled freedom for Blacks, at a cost of only "a Winchester, a frying pan, and $15.00 to file."[25]

Charismatic Black separatist leaders, troops of evangelical recruiting agents dispatched to the South, and White Republican support failed to attract enough Blacks. McCabe's vision of creating a Black-dominated enclave within the Oklahoma Territory foundered.

McCabe met with fierce resistance, both within and beyond the borders of Oklahoma. In Oklahoma, Whites objected. Some Blacks thought the idea fanciful. Native Americans feared how they would fare under in a Black-led state.

Elsewhere, White southerners, fearing the loss of cheap Black labor, crafted a propaganda campaign aimed at retaining Blacks and even wooing back expatriates. They claimed that Oklahoma land was unsuitable for farmers—a damning indictment to a largely agrarian group of southern Blacks.

McCabe's putative allies, politicians in the ardent Republican's own party, questioned whether a Black state could exist in the absence of a constitutional amendment. First, they pondered the implications of creating a state wherein no Whites possessed title to land. Next, they worried about the "dual status" of Blacks, since presumably Blacks in this idealized all-Black state would be vested with full citizenship rights, yet had no such privileges should they venture into another state. In the final analysis, however, the decisive issue proved less arcane. It became simply a question of numbers: far too few Blacks migrated to the Oklahoma Territory during the ten land openings between 1889 and 1906.[26] Whites outnumbered them physically and dominated them politically.

A Black-Indian axis might have held White domination in check. Such an alliance, though perhaps politically expedient and shrewd, never materialized. Blacks empathized with Indian suffering at the hands of Whites, but resented the Indians' relatively superior social status. S. Douglas Russell, then in Langston, beseeched the leaders of the Indian nations to consider aligning themselves with Blacks. He argued that "negroes and Indians would have the political balance of power in the future state of Oklahoma, provided those votes would form a solid, undivided phalanx at the polls."[27] But Indians, including those tribes who had once openly welcomed Blacks into the fold, began to distance themselves from Blacks. The insidious anti-Black views of southern Whites had infested Oklahoma and metastasized. Indians sacrificed political self-interest at the altar of southern-style racism.

Undeterred by the low numbers and the politics of division, McCabe soon made it known that he wished to become the appointed governor of the Oklahoma Territory, whether or not it became a Black state. Proponents of the "Black state" idea went to hundreds of Black migrants in Alabama, Atlanta, Georgia, and other locations to promote his appointment. Supportive Republicans organized efforts by Blacks all over the nation to assist McCabe. For example, prominent Blacks in Little Rock, Arkansas, received a circular on March 11, 1890, urging Black solidarity:

> As Mr. McCabe has no colored opponent … we urge you to prepare at once a strong petition, and have every loyal colored citizen to sign it and forward the same direct to President Harrison as early as possible, as the appointment for the Territorial offices may be sent to the Senate at an early date, and we trust you will give the matter your serious and prompt attention, and receive the lasting gratitude of this committee and 22,000 colored citizens of Oklahoma.[28]

However, the negative reaction to McCabe's candidacy came swiftly and certainly. Many proclaimed publicly what others only muttered privately. The price for McCabe's prize would be steep. He would be a marked man were he to become governor.[29]

Still, McCabe and the Oklahoma Immigration Society continued the promotional blitz as new lands opened in Oklahoma Territory. On September 22, 1891, some 868,414 acres of Sac and Fox, Iowa, and Shawnee-Pottawatomie lands opened. The government had negotiated agreements with the Indians whereby each individual received an allotment and the remainder of the reservation became open for settlers as part of Oklahoma Territory. The *Norman Transcript* reported on McCabe's approach to these new opportunities:

> A Negro secret order at Langston City, near Guthrie, has 850 agents in southern states advising Negroes to come and join them in obtaining homes as a colony in the new territory to be opened—by force if necessary. They care for families arriving, awaiting any opening of lands and are armed.
>
> In the meantime:
>
> A movement is on foot to colonize with negroes the Indian lands soon to be thrown open to general settlement. The movement has its origin at Langston City, a negro settlement not far from here. Thousands of letters have seen sent out with this object in view. Today at a meeting, a resolution was adopted that, from the most reliable information the new lands will speedily be opened; 'that we notify our people the colored citizens of the south, to be here on the 10th of September, and that those who intend to drive through the Indian country, to start at once; and that the 850 Langston agents throughout the southern states notify the people of the importance of being here by the 10th of September, to join us in assuring homes in the new lands.'
>
> As a result of the work of the Langston agents, hundreds of negroes have already gone to Langston and are being cared for by their colored friends until the time for the invasion arrives. Many negroes are arriving daily, and by the time the lands are proclaimed open to settlement, it is believed that thousands of colored people will have to take part in the race for homes. The Langston people believed that the negroes are armed....The organization is secret, and until today its objects and plans have been known to none but the members.[30]

Though somewhat successful in settling the lands opened from the land holding of the Sac and Fox, Iowa, and Shawnee-Pottawatomie, Blacks would be less successful in subsequent openings.

McCabe's disappointments mounted. First, Republican Party leaders in the nation's capital nixed his appointment as territorial governor. Instead, Governor Cassius Barnes appointed him assistant territorial auditor, a position he retained until Democrats took control of the new state's legislature in the year of Oklahoma statehood, 1907. Next, Black migration to the state plummeted. The years of anti-migration campaigning worked. The cost of migration, the loss of family and community ties, fear of the unknown, and uncertainly about the suitability of Oklahoma land for farming all caused consternation among Blacks. Rather than branch out into Oklahoma, many chose to stay rooted in the Deep South. The Black population crested at about 10 percent.

Defeated but undaunted, McCabe now turned his attention to the creation of Black towns in the Twin Territories of Oklahoma. Here, he found phenomenal success. The concept of an all-Black town appealed to Blacks for a number of reasons: (1) the psychic security of living among one's "own kind"; (2) the opportunity for political and economic self-determination; (3) the prospect of a buffer or a safe haven from race-based hate groups such as the Ku Klux Klan; (4) the chance to prove their worth to White Americans; and (5) the possibility of an escape from the affirmative social hostility exhibited by some Indians and many Whites toward them.[31]

Scene in Nicodemus, 1885.

—Courtesy the Kansas State Historical Society
Library & Archives Division

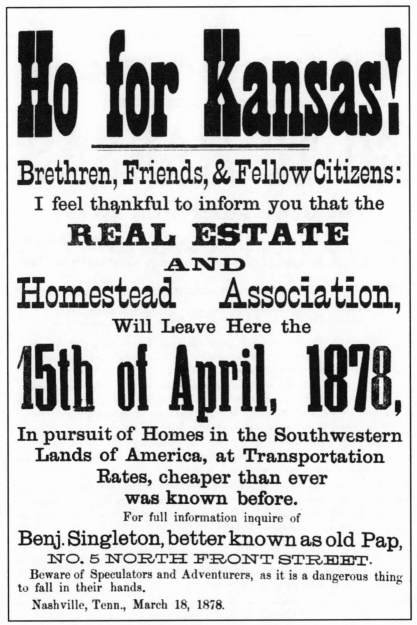

Circular for Kansas migration, 1878.

—Courtesy the Kansas State Historical Society
Library & Archives Division

All Colored People

THAT WANT TO

GO TO KANSAS,

On September 5th, 1877,

Can do so for $5.00

IMMIGRATION.

WHEREAS, We, the colored people of Lexington, Ky,. knowing that there is an abundance of choice lands now belonging to the Government, have assembled ourselves together for the purpose of locating on said lands. Therefore,

BE IT RESOLVED, That we do now organize ourselves into a Colony, as follows:— Any person wishing to become a member of this Colony can do so by paying the sum of one dollar ($1.00), and this money is to be paid by the first of September, 1877, in instalments of twenty-five cents at a time, or otherwise as may be desired.

RESOLVED, That this Colony has agreed to consolidate itself with the Nicodemus Towns, Solomon Valley, Graham County, Kansas, and can only do so by entering the vacant lands now in their midst, which costs $5.00.

RESOLVED, That this Colony shall consist of seven officers—President, Vice-President, Secretary, Treasurer, and three Trustees. President—M. M. Bell; Vice-President —Isaac Talbott; Secretary—W. J. Niles; Treasurer—Daniel Clarke; Trustees—Jerry Lee, William Jones, and Abner Webster.

RESOLVED, That this Colony shall have from one to two hundred militia, more or less, as the case may require, to keep peace and order, and any member failing to pay in his dues, as aforesaid, or failing to comply with the above rules in any particular, will not be recognized or protected by the Colony.

Circular for Kansas migration, 1877.

—Courtesy the Kansas State Historical Society
Library & Archives Division